KING & COURT
David Loades

H enry looked every inch a king. At the age of 18 he was head and shoulders taller than his courtiers, with a ruddy colouring and a magnificent physique which he had inherited from his maternal grandfather, Edward IV. Expectations ran high. His tutor John Skelton had 'acquaint[ed] him with the muses nine', giving him a first-rate classical and biblical education. Although a protective father had prevented him from jousting in public, he had received an excellent grounding in the martial arts, and was a good tennis player and a keen huntsman.

Henry was quite intelligent enough to realize his own limitations, and one of his first actions as king in 1509 was to confirm Henry VII's councillors and senior servants in their posts. Nevertheless, this did not signify a continuity of policy. Thomas More, who must have known something of Henry's mind, hailed him as the monarch who would repair the Crown's relations with the nobility – which his father had notoriously damaged – and within a matter of weeks two of Henry VII's most unpopular financial 'policemen' were on their way to the block. The rejoicing was universal: '… everything is full of milk and honey and nectar,' wrote Lord Mountjoy. 'Avarice has fled the country. Our king is not after gold, or gems or precious metals, but virtue, glory, immortality.' It soon transpired that this glory was to be sought on the battlefield, and that it would be by war that he would repair his relations with the aristocracy, but for the moment it was the humanists and other scholars who sang his praises most loudly.

Almost the first thing he did, which took all the politicians by surprise, was to marry his brother Arthur's widow, the 25-year-old Catherine of Aragon, who had been lurking unhappily about the Court since the prince's death seven years before. Although Henry badly wanted the friendship of her father, King Ferdinand, this seems also to have been a love match, and the newly-weds were crowned together on Midsummer Day. 'The end of sadness and the beginning of joy,' wrote Thomas More with more enthusiasm than foresight. Henry was to prove a passionate king, and at first that was entirely positive. He set out to present himself to the world as a Renaissance prince, with all the appropriate splendour, and it was this splendour which dictated the style of his Court, and in the manner in which

ABOVE:
The Crown and the Tudor rose.

FRONT COVER:
This portrait by Joos van Cleeve shows the 44-year-old king as rather more youthful than he would have been in life.

FRONT COVER BACKGROUND:
Hampton Court Palace.

LEFT:
This unusual portrait, which is alleged to be of Henry VIII, shows him as he would have appeared at the time of the Field of Cloth of Gold, 1520.

'This magnificent, excellent and triumphant Court.'
A FOREIGN AMBASSADOR ON VISITING HENRY VIII'S COURT

RIGHT:

A view of Hampton
Court from the gardens,
showing the Tudor
palace as it would
have appeared before
William III's
re-building in the
seventeenth century.

The sheer splendour of the Court was never greater than at Hampton Court Palace. Hampton Court outshone Henry's many other houses and rivalled the great palaces of Europe in style, opulence, decoration and in its many treasures. Here life mirrored the rise in the king's power and influence at home and abroad.

Henry had more houses than he knew what to do with. At various times he held as many as 69, and in any given year about 45. Some he inherited, some he bought and some came to him through the treason of their owners, or the dissolution of the monasteries. Some he sold and some he granted away. Each of his queens in turn received two or three. The more remote ones, like the king's manor in Newcastle or Parlaunt in Gloucestershire, he never visited, and some of the smaller houses were mere hunting lodges. A few, like Minster Lovell in Oxfordshire, were kept up but not used. The majority were concentrated in the Home Counties and were used on the regular migrations of the Court. Only a few were great palaces, capable of holding the whole establishment, and many of the household were left behind when the king was using one of his smaller residences.

BELOW RIGHT:

The grand west gate
of Hampton Court
Palace – a part of
Henry VIII's extensive
building programme.

FAR RIGHT CENTRE:

A fine example
of Renaissance
craftsmanship: the
astronomical clock
on Anne Boleyn's
gateway at Hampton
Court Palace.

FAR RIGHT BOTTOM:

Nonsuch Palace as it
appeared after Henry's
death, showing clearly
the resemblance to
the French chateau of
Chambord. Henry spent
a fortune building and
furnishing Nonsuch.

Henry's earliest favourite was Greenwich Palace, where he had been born, and which was large enough for all eventualities, but after he acquired Hampton Court Palace from Cardinal Wolsey in 1528, that became the most used. Between 1529 and 1538 the king spent over £46,000 (about £46 million in modern money) on building the State Apartments, the Chapel, the Hall and the Great Kitchen, all of which survive today. Most of the Base Court and the Clock Court are also of Henry's building, although parts of his palace were swept away in the great reconstruction which took place in the time of William III. Like the other great houses, Hampton Court was laid out with a 'King's Side' and a 'Queen's Side', and equipped with tennis courts and a tiltyard. It was also surrounded by carefully planned gardens, some of which have been reconstructed, and had a Home Park, where the ladies could be entertained with a little light hunting. Henry's other (slightly later)

extravagance was Nonsuch in Surrey, built from scratch in imitation of the chateau of Chambord, Francis I's palace on the Loire. There he spent £25,000 between 1538 and 1545, but it was never finished in his lifetime and was demolished in the late seventeenth century. Whitehall, which came to the Crown on Wolsey's fall in 1529, was another great house which was extensively used because of its convenience for Westminster.

All these palaces were as much for show as for use, and their size and grandeur were commented upon in awed tones by both domestic and foreign visitors.

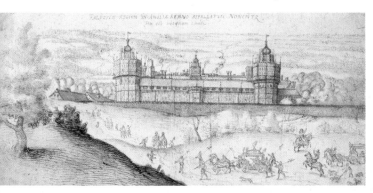

A number of the king's building accounts survive, particularly for Hampton Court, and these give a unique insight into the King's Office of Works. St James's Palace was built between 1531 and 1536, probably as a London residence for Henry's illegitimate son, the Duke of Richmond, who died there in the latter year.

The Royal Household

Henry gathered around him a crowded throng of people enjoying the privileges and pleasures of Court life, and enduring its dangers. The Court was divided into two sections, below stairs and above stairs. In the first place was the domestic household, which supported everyday life. This consisted of about 30 departments and sub-departments, such as the kitchen and the woodyard, and was controlled by the Lord Steward, under whom worked the Comptroller and the accounts office, known as the Counting House. Each department was run by a Sergeant, and its staff might vary from three or four to upwards of 50. Only the Steward and the Comptroller ranked as gentlemen. The Sergeants were yeomen, and the remainder artisans or labourers. The household was very hierarchical and promotion went by seniority. Positions were much in demand and vacancies were filled in theory by the Lord Steward, but in practice usually by the departmental Sergeants. The servants were overwhelmingly male, only the more senior living in the vicinity with their wives; the majority 'lived in' which created disciplinary problems, particularly over prostitution.

ABOVE: *This painting of an anonymous gentleman, attributed to Hans Eworth and painted in about 1546, depicts a courtier in full dress.*

LEFT: *Catherine of Aragon in middle age (c.1530), after the breakdown of her 21-year marriage to Henry.*

ABOVE: *An unknown Court lady, thought to be Mary Zouch, drawn in about 1538. Scores of similar drawings were made by Hans Holbein of English courtiers.*

The Court proper – where the king was to be found – was called the Chamber and was controlled by the Lord Chamberlain. Here the king and queen were surrounded by noble and gentle servants, and all business and ceremonial were conducted. In the Chamber the king's advisers met and ambassadors were received. This was the focus of the Court's magnificence. Its culture, music, elaborate entertainments and festivities were all functions of the Chamber, and presented in a way which spared neither luxury nor expense. The king's and queen's wardrobes, in which were made and stored the jewelled and embroidered clothes which the royal couple habitually wore, were attached to the Chamber, as were the Gentlemen Pensioners, the Yeomen of the Guard (the royal bodyguard), the physicians, chaplains and confessors. The Chamber was the heart of the king's *maiestas* – the centre of his honour and prestige.

Control was much more informal than in the household, but the comings and goings of the courtiers about their regular duties had to be licensed by the Chamberlain, and it was a serious matter to leave the Court without permission. Many of these gentlemen servants were part-timers, one of whose functions was to keep the Court in touch with their counties of residence. The queen had a separate Chamber, the staff of which was largely female, and formed a useful balance to the king's all-male establishment. Henry also had a small group of chosen companions who formed his Privy Chamber, and these men were the closest to him, both personally and politically. They ran his private errands, and were not under the direct control of the Chamberlain. The king chose them, and disciplined them as he pleased.

ABOVE:

Henry reading in his bedchamber, an image from a Latin psalter made for him. Henry was well-read and learned; he had a large collection of books which he annotated industriously.

LEFT: A walnut writing box or table desk, probably English (1525–27), of the kind which would have been used by Henry VIII when travelling.

5

Royal Pastimes

RIGHT:

Hunting boar and hares with dogs, a scene set in Italy. In England the usual quarry was the stag. Henry was an avid hunter all his life.

RIGHT:

A sixteenth-century tournament, typical of the many in which Henry VIII engaged. This represents the fatal encounter of Henri II of France with Count Montgomery in 1559.

The pastimes which Henry pursued most enthusiastically were hunting and hawking. Stables, kennels and toils (for hawks) were maintained on a lavish scale, each controlled by a Master or Keeper and staffed by dozens of servants. The Master of the King's Horse was an important courtier. As a young man, Henry hunted at all seasons, choosing his game appropriately, and an invitation to join his party was a high honour. As he grew older he went out less often, but continued the chase until he was no longer able to sit astride his horse. As a young man he also jousted with skill and enthusiasm, often choosing his companions for their aptitude in that sport. In spite of his warlike zeal, this was the nearest he ever came to actual fighting; however, he was directly responsible for maintaining the essentially medieval code of chivalry which these tournaments represented. Real war fascinated him from a distance. He designed ships, experimented with guns, and studied docks and fortifications, surrounding himself with experts in all these skills.

In a more peaceful vein, he entertained scholars and theologians, such as Thomas Cranmer, collected books and prided himself upon his biblical knowledge. His Court was also celebrated for its masques and revels. The former were elaborate mimes, like the assault on the Green Castle in 1525, where the (female) defenders pelted their assailants with fruit and flowers before, inevitably, surrendering to the dance. Such play-acting sometimes had a point, as in 1536 when during an anti-papal pageant a boatload of mock cardinals was spilled into the River Thames by the King's Men.

Privately Henry played the game which is now known as real (royal) tennis and, like most of his courtiers, gambled compulsively. At the former he was generally successful but not, apparently, at the latter. Unfortunately his privy purse expenses only record what was paid out when he lost, so we do not know how much he may have won. However, the king's most controversial pastime was Courtly Love, in which he continued to indulge until about 1540. These episodes were supposed to be harmless charades, intended to enhance the status (and tickle the vanity) of the ladies of the Court. However, in such an overheated atmosphere they could easily – and sometimes did – get out of hand.

ABOVE: A fanfare to open the great Westminster tournament of January 1511.

BELOW: A suit of armour made for the king about 1515, with a horse armour, probably by Flemish or Italian craftsmen. The suit is lavishly engraved with the emblems of Henry and Catherine of Aragon.

Henry's personal piety was consistently orthodox and strict. He considered himself, rightly, to be a competent theologian and biblical scholar. He was also compulsively self-righteous, and persuaded himself that whatever course of action he chose with regard to the Church was morally and politically justified. He broke with Rome in 1534, convinced that the Pope was seeking jurisdiction to which he was not entitled, and dissolved the monasteries equally convinced that the religious life had become unworthy and corrupt. In choosing these courses he was, to some extent, following the humanist priorities which he had absorbed in his youth. Many humanists were hostile to the papacy, and to what they regarded as 'superstitious practices'. Henry, however, remained consistently loyal to the sacraments of the Church, particularly the mass, and when evangelical preachers began to attack those sacraments in the later 1530s he reacted strongly. Throughout the changes which his policies brought about he remained true to his own idiosyncratic vision.

Religion divided the Court, at first over the Royal Supremacy, and when that had been successfully enforced, over the activities of the evangelicals. There were 'conservative' and 'reforming' groups within the Chamber, and even within the Privy Chamber, and each of the king's marriages resulted in shifts in the balance between them. Catherine of Aragon resisted all pressure to conform; Anne Boleyn favoured the evangelicals; Catherine Howard the conservatives; and Catherine Parr nearly came to grief for her reforming sympathies. The prevailing climate of the Court could be judged, not so much from the Chapel Royal (where the liturgy and the music alike remained traditional and magnificent) as from the preachers chosen for special occasions.

As a young man, Henry went on pilgrimages and performed all the rites expected of him diligently, if not enthusiastically. Later his emphasis changed and he became much more scripturally orientated, going so far as to authorize the translation of the Bible into English. Nevertheless, he retained a horror of Lutheran 'heresies' to the end of his life, and his courtiers had to tread extremely carefully to make sure that they conformed to 'the king's proceedings'. Throughout all the changes which followed 1533, Henry remained loyal to his reforming archbishop, Thomas Cranmer, even when he knew that his policies would cause Cranmer distress, and personally rescued him from at least two conservative plots. The Chapel Royal, with its staff of singing men, choristers and chaplains, remained the showplace of the royal piety and courtiers were expected to attend, whatever their confessional allegiance.

Food Fit for a King

When thinking of any sixteenth-century menus it is worth remembering that there were no refrigerators and no freezers. This meant that fresh fruit and vegetables were only available in season, and that perishable commodities such as meat and fish had to be bought as needed and consumed quickly. The Court ate vast quantities of meat and huge numbers of game birds. The former was bought 'on the hoof' and slaughtered in a special department of the household called the acatry.

By the time of Henry's reign, collective meals in the Great Hall were things of the past except on special occasions. The king and queen normally ate in the Privy Chamber, accompanied by their invited guests, and waited on by the Privy Chamber servants. Meanwhile the head officers (such as the Lord Chamberlain) kept their tables in the Presence Chamber, accompanied by their respective staffs, and waited on by Chamber servants. Only the menial servants still gathered in the Hall. During Henry's reign this pattern was increasingly disrupted by the habit of noblemen and gentlemen drawing their rations from the buttery, and having them prepared and eaten in their private apartments. This growing practice was easily tolerated as far as breakfast and supper were concerned, but was frowned upon for dinner (normally taken in mid-morning) because it diminished the social opportunities of the meal.

ABOVE RIGHT:

A collection of Tudor utensils assembled in a corner of the Great Kitchen at Hampton Court Palace. It includes pots, jars, baskets, and a pestle and mortar for pounding herbs and spices.

RIGHT:

The banqueting hall built by Henry at Leeds Castle in Kent. Leeds was a royal castle but not visited very often. The Court was here in May 1522.

ABOVE: *Meat from a hare being prepared in a kitchen. In royal palaces such work was done in the acatry before the prepared meat was sent to the kitchen.*

BELOW: *The Burghley Nef. This magnificent salt cellar in the form of a trading ship was made in France in 1527. It would have been typical of the tableware used at courtly banquets.*

Routine meals consisted of several different kinds of meat (or fish if it was a fast day), soups and sweetmeats. Root vegetables such as carrots and onions were used as embellishments, and salads in season. Potatoes were unknown and rice was rare and exotic. Fine bread was served to the royal family and the gentry, coarse bread to the rest; and all washed down with copious draughts of ale (unfortified by hops) and wine. The wine was imported from France and the cellar was one of the household's major departments. Water was unsafe and considered fit only for horses. Banquets were ornate, featuring pies and pastries, sweet puddings, syllabubs and other confections, together with the sauces which were lavishly applied to all dishes, sweet or savoury. Plates and dishes of silver, pewter and wood were in regular use by this time. Food was eaten with a knife and with the left hand, hence the need for finger bowls and towels; forks were only introduced at the end of the sixteenth century. Food for the royal table was cooked in the Privy Kitchen, while that for the Chamber and the Hall emanated from the Great Kitchen. There was much competition to be fed from the Privy Kitchen and bribery was not unknown.

ABOVE: *Anne of Cleves by Holbein (1539). This is the portrait which misled Henry into expecting a beauty for his fourth wife.*

ABOVE: *Tudor wine flagon, dated about 1548. Known as the 'Parr Pot', it bears the arms of Sir William Parr, uncle of Catherine.*

RIGHT: *Court musicians playing pipe and tabor, trumpet, harp and cithern; from a Latin psalter produced for the king. Henry's orchestra, The King's Music, was the finest in Europe.*

enry notoriously married six times and, apart from the years 1537–40 and 1542–43, there was always a queen in England. Each in turn was given an endowment of between £3,000 and £4,500 a year, out of which she was expected to pay her servants and keep up the properties which had been allocated to her. She was also expected to be generous with rewards to those who sought her favour, and in pious benefactions to religious foundations and the poor.

Within the Court her Chamber was a foil to the king's. Although most of her officers would have been men – and usually safely married – her regular companions and many of her servants would have been female. These ladies were essential for the civilized image of the Court, and for its masques and entertainments, most of which involved dancing. Many of them were unmarried,

and sometimes very young, because the Queen's Chamber was the most desirable 'display cabinet' for the aristocratic marriage market, and competition for places among courtier families was intense. They were also much in demand as partners in the game of Courtly Love, wherein unattached (usually) males made a great show of their undying devotion, and bombarded the objects of their affections with poems and small gifts. The ladies responded with coy encouragement or fierce disdain – usually simulated – which provoked their swains to further efforts. The game had originated with the troubadours, and in the desire to elevate the status of women by making them objects of unattainable desire, but it could have dangerous effects, particularly if the king was a player!

Every Queen's Chamber reflected her family and her personality. Catherine of Aragon retained a number of Spanish servants, and insisted on the highest level of orthodox piety. Anne Boleyn was a politician in her own right, and interested herself in foreign affairs. Anne of Cleves kept a miniature Rhineland Court, and Catherine Parr presided over a kind of theological seminar, much to her husband's concern. All, however, were expected to pursue the 'female arts', particularly needlework and gossip. This latter could be dangerous, and it was the chatter of her ladies which undid Anne Boleyn when the political climate of the Court turned against her. Only Catherine Howard tried to use her Chamber as a smokescreen to conceal her own indiscretions, and that proved fatal to her Chief Lady of the Bedchamber, Jane Rochford, as well as to herself. Women did not, on the whole, play a leading part in the affairs of Church or State, but each of Henry's marriages was a political statement, and his sexuality a factor of prime importance.

Henry's last queen, Catherine Parr; a portrait by Court painter Master John, made around the time of her wedding to Henry in 1543.

The Travelling Court

enry's Court was constantly on the move. Given the primitive state of hygiene in sixteenth-century England, upwards of a thousand people could not inhabit one building, however magnificent, for long periods without a break. Even great palaces like Greenwich or Hampton Court needed to be cleaned and 'aired' after a month or so. So the king moved in a stately orbit, early in his reign from Greenwich to Richmond, Bridewell and Eltham, and later on from Greenwich to Hampton Court or Whitehall, with occasional excursions to Nonsuch, Windsor or New Hall, Essex. These moves were regular and familiar, and the courtiers and servants knew which rooms they would occupy and how their duties would be discharged. The Chapel Royal, for instance, did not travel to Windsor, because there was already a chapel establishment there which performed the same function. Sometimes the Court travelled a little further afield, to Oatlands in Surrey or Woodstock in Oxfordshire, and then both the household and the Chamber would be reduced to fit the houses. However, these were also regular ports of call, and did not require much thought or effort to organize.

A royal progress, however, was different. Although they often started and finished in familiar houses, these were deliberately intended to take the king out of his 'comfort zone', to show himself to his people, and for these careful itineraries or 'geists' were prepared. Henry did not normally go far: Kent, Wiltshire or Hampshire usually represented the extent of his ambition. His visits to Calais in 1520 and to York in 1541 were altogether exceptional. However, on progress the Court did not normally use royal residences. Sometimes the king stayed with senior noblemen or officials, and sometimes in episcopal or monastic residences. For instance, in July 1517 he spent five days with the Bishop of Winchester at Farnham Castle, and in August of the same year visited the Abbeys of Beaulieu and Christchurch. Very often only the royal couple and their most intimate servants could be accommodated at the main house, and the royal harbingers (or accommodation officers) had the onerous job of finding lodgings for other courtiers and servants somewhere in the vicinity. This happened when Henry stayed at Sir Thomas Lovell's residence at Enfield, Middlesex, in July 1518. In an inauspicious place, like Castle Acre Priory in Norfolk (October 1522), these might be scattered over several miles of countryside.

ABOVE: *A nineteenth-century portrayal of Henry and Anne Boleyn hunting with crossbows in Windsor Forest.*

In such circumstances the Chamber service was heavily reduced: only a few advisers, for instance, travelled with the Court – the rest remained in London – and the household might be represented by no more than a few cooks. Sometimes the king made use of his host's servants, but very often the host and his household had moved out to give the Court a free run, and this seems to have been what Henry preferred. Progresses were not holidays and business continued to be transacted as usual. During Wolsey's time in power, he never accompanied the king on progress, but always tracked the itinerary closely, trying to make sure that he was never more than a day's ride (about 20 miles) away, so that he was always ready to answer a summons if it should come.

In the early part of the reign the king and queen might travel separately, because their business was different. Henry tried to include as much hunting as possible, while Catherine went on pilgrimage to the shrines along their route, in which case the queen might have her own 'geists', and stay in different residences. Henry was not a 'saddle king', constantly on the move, in the medieval sense, but he did occasionally take off in an unpredictable fashion, especially if there was plague in the vicinity, and his officers had to be ready to gratify his whims.

ABOVE: Queen Catherine of Aragon at prayer; a stained-glass window (c.1524) from the Tudor chapel at The Vyne in Berkshire.

The Court was no longer a centre of administration, departments such as the Exchequer and Chancery having moved out in the twelfth century, but it was the centre of politics because of its proximity to the king. Only the monarch could resolve the quarrels and disputes which arose among his advisers, and that brought them on to the stage of the Court, even if they had nothing to do with it. It was claimed, for instance, that Wolsey's fall was brought about by courtiers who denied him access to the king when he was already in disfavour. That was not the case. He fell from power because he had failed to meet Henry's expectations. Wolsey was not himself a courtier, but he knew the importance of keeping trusted men about the king, and that network failed him when the crisis arose. Thomas Cromwell also fell because he forfeited the king's confidence for political reasons. Both he and Wolsey had survived the hostility of courtiers for years. Only the king mattered. Political scandals were numerous and matched every twist of the king's policies, from the purge of the Privy Chamber in 1519 to the destruction of the Duke of Norfolk in 1546.

ABOVE: *Anne Boleyn, a portrait showing her at about the time of her marriage to Henry. The king proposed to Anne in 1527 but they were not able to marry until January 1533.*

LEFT:
Henry Fitzroy, Duke of Richmond, Henry's only acknowledged illegitimate son. A miniature by Lucas Horenbout painted c.1534.

RIGHT:
A portrait by Holbein of a young lady, thought to be Catherine Howard – Henry's fifth queen – who paid the ultimate penalty for her extra-marital affairs.

ABOVE: *Mary Boleyn, Anne's elder sister and Henry's mistress, c.1520–25, in a portrait which expresses her reputation for beauty and docility.*

Sexual scandals were less numerous, but could explode with fearsome power. Matchmaking was endemic, and might involve indiscreet behaviour, but was hardly ever scandalous. The queen's young ladies were strictly chaperoned by the Chief Gentlewoman – invariably a matron of experience. It was not a scandal when the king took a mistress, and only the queen was outraged when Elizabeth Blount produced Henry Fitzroy in 1519. The first real crisis came in 1515 when Henry's sister Mary, recently widowed by Louis XII of France, seduced Charles Brandon, the Duke of Suffolk, who had been sent to bring her home. Brandon was one of the king's most trusted friends, but it took him a long time (and a lot of money) to buy off Henry's displeasure at his marriage. The fall of Anne Boleyn amidst allegations of infidelity was, in fact, political. She was destroyed by her enemies using scandal as a weapon, because that was the nature of her hold over Henry. The king was a passionate but suggestible lover, whose lust could, by using the right accusations, be turned to loathing. The only scandal in the proper sense was that which destroyed Henry's fifth queen, Catherine Howard. Catherine was an experienced young lady, who found her ageing husband boring and took herself off to other beds. This was treason because of the threat to the legitimacy of her children, and she paid with her life. Henry was shattered by her infidelities, which marked the passing of his virility.

European Influences

enry's Court was international in two senses. In the first place the king and his consorts employed a lot of foreign servants. Catherine of Aragon had Spanish confessors, apothecaries and physicians, as well as quite a number of ladies. Anne Boleyn kept up her French connections, and some of Anne of Cleves' most trusted servants were German. Henry supported French and Flemish musicians, Flemish and German artists, like Lucas Horenbout and Hans Holbein, and Italian scholars. Towards the end of his reign he employed the Frenchman Jean Rotz as his hydrographer, with responsibility for surveying all his harbours.

It was also a European Court in the sense of sharing a common culture. The normal language used was English, but most courtiers spoke good French, and both Italian and Latin were in common use – the latter particularly with visiting clergy. The chivalric tradition, represented by tournaments, 'disguisings' (plays or mimes in costume) and Courtly Love, was borrowed originally from the fifteenth-century Court of Burgundy, while the whole notion of a Privy Chamber was modelled on its French equivalent. The fact that England and France were intermittently at war made no difference to this trade in ideas.

Fashion was also international, then as now. Ladies styles, in particular, might be derived from French, Flemish or Spanish originals, according to the make up of the Queen's Chamber, or the political orientation of the regime in general. For some reason,

RIGHT:

An original score of Henry's composition 'Pastime with good company'. Henry was proud of his accomplishment as a composer.

FAR RIGHT:

A fictional courtly dance involving Henry, Anne Boleyn, the Duke and Duchess of Suffolk, and Henry's elder sister, Margaret, the dowager Queen of Scots. Greenwich Palace is in the background.

perhaps because of their unfamiliarity, German styles were not considered becoming, which was another reason why Anne of Cleves found herself in difficulties.

The music performed was mostly English, partly because Henry fancied himself as a composer, but the dances in favour varied like the fashions in clothes. The king might spend as much as a third of his ordinary income on his Court (£49,000 in 1546–47), largely because he was playing in a competitive league. For most of his reign judicious observers (such as the Venetians) reckoned that the magnificence of his Court excelled those of Spain or the Empire, but lagged behind that of France. This was no mean achievement for a king whose resources were only a fraction of those of Charles V or Francis I, and contributed significantly to the honour by which he set such great store. A king's glory might lie primarily on the battlefield, but it was also reflected in the splendour of his Court.

ABOVE:

Henry VIII arriving for his meeting with the King of France at the Field of Cloth of Gold in June 1520. This flamboyant and extravagant meeting between the English and the French Courts in the Val d'Or, outside Calais, was unsurpassed in splendour. Guisnes Castle can be seen in the background.

LEFT:

Francis I of France, by Jean Clouet, c.1525, showing him much as he would have looked at the Field of Cloth of Gold.

To the modern descendants of his subjects, Henry is best known as the king who married six times and executed two of his wives. He is, according to the prejudices of the historian, either a tyrant – with whose colossal ego no woman was able to cope, the man who ruined the Church and executed his ministers and servants according to the whim of the moment, or he is a great king – the creator of parliamentary sovereignty, the Church of England and the Royal Navy. The truth is that both these pictures are accurate – up to a point. In one sense, and particularly in his attitude to war and chivalry, he was the last of the medieval kings; but at the same time in his perception of national sovereignty, and of the nobility as servants of the state, he belonged to a recognizably modern world. He did have a great ego and was compulsively self-righteous, which made him erratic and very difficult to deal with, by both men and women. Towards the end of his life constant pain and physical frustration also gave him an explosive and unpredictable temper, which taxed the resources of all those who had to deal with him.